S0-DJZ-406

IOWA from the Sky

© Sharon Rexroth 2005

All rights reserved. No part of this book may be reproduced or transmitted in any form or by any means, electronic or mechanically, except by a reviewer who may quote brief passages in a review to be printed in a magazine or newspaper.

Quixote Press
800-571-2665

Dedicated to....

The author's parents and parents-in-law all grew up in Iowa. Because of their strong, positive influence, this book is dedicated to them:

Earl and Alice Paasch
Allen and Ninita Rexroth

The book is also dedicated to a supportive and loving family ...... husband, Tom, children, Jinjer, Jason, Joel and Jena, and grandchildren, Jacob and Ben Durbin, Jaxon and Jevin Rexroth, Tyler Rexroth and Kelynn, Jada and Liberty Wright.

May all who read "Iowa from the Sky" know that Iowa is a wonderful blend of culture, values, tradition and educational opportunities!

Enjoy!

Special Thanks to....

Marcia Rigsby, Pamela Manley, Teri Rexroth, Karen Timmerman, Tom Rexroth, Bruce Carlson and Lee-Ann and Richard Paasch.

Hi, my name is Barnaby!
I'm a goldfinch and
Iowa is my favorite place to be.

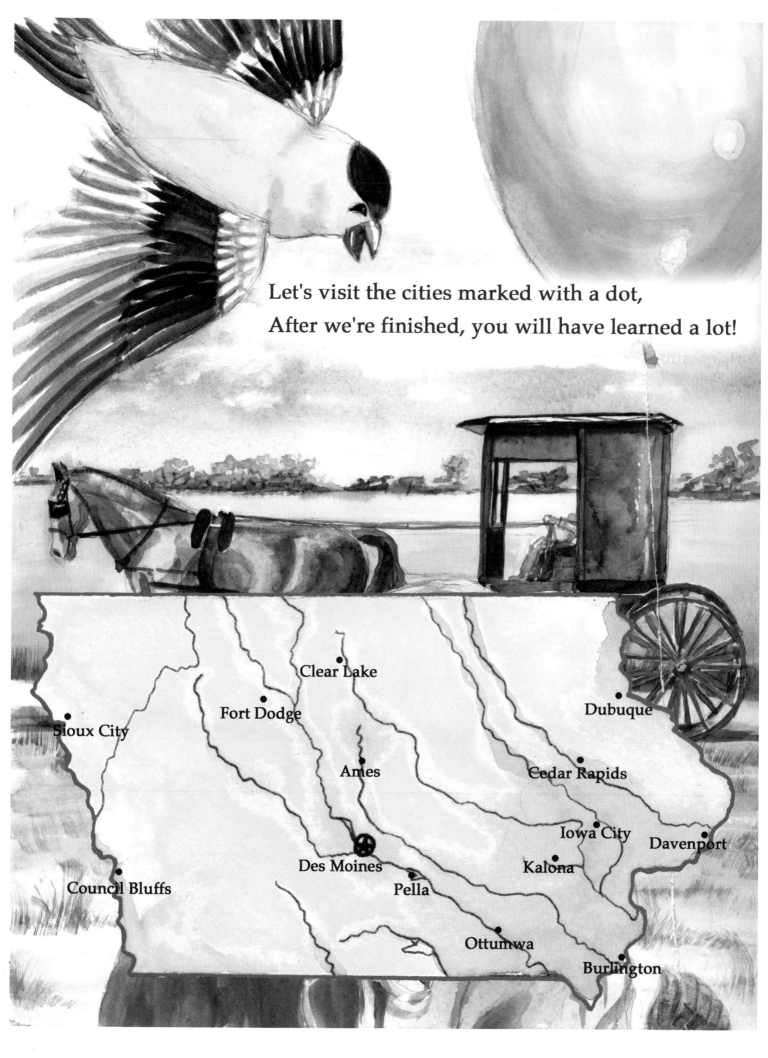

Let's visit the cities marked with a dot,
After we're finished, you will have learned a lot!

Clear Lake

Fort Dodge

Dubuque

Sioux City

Ames

Cedar Rapids

Iowa City

Davenport

Des Moines

Kalona

Council Bluffs

Pella

Ottumwa

Burlington

It's fun to fly over Iowa,
　　if you're a bird.
To fly as a person,
　　without a plane, would be absurd!
Because I can see
　　all over the Hawkeye state,
I can convince you
　　that Iowa is really great!

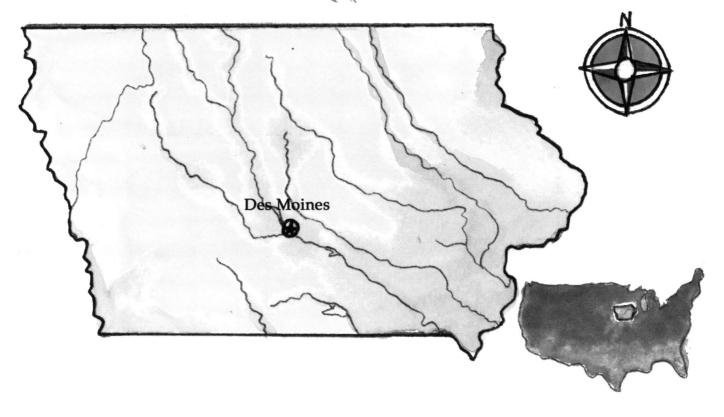

Des Moines

State tree: Oak

State Flower: Wild Rose

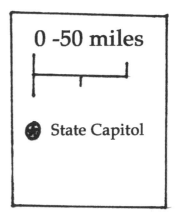

0 -50 miles

State Capitol

Des Moines

One of my favorite places to go,
Is Des Moines, where you can shop,
go to the zoo or see a show.

There in the dome where laws are made for the people,
The dome is gold and round, not like a steeple.

When I am tired
and want to rest,
I fly over to Pella
where I can build my nest.

Pella is home to many
who call themselves "Dutch".
They traveled from the Netherlands
to Iowa which they like very much!

While there, I enjoy
the tulips blooming in Spring,
When they scrub down the streets
'til they're really clean!

Ottumwa

Another one of my favorite spots
   in my favorite state,
Is Ottumwa, near a great big lake!
Lake Rathbun is one of the biggest lakes
   in the state I love best,
I love to race through the sky
   chasing sailboats before I rest.

Burlington

Then I travel on eastward
to a town on the Mississippi River.
It's Burlington, Iowa's first
territorial capitol ever.

Burlington has beautiful homes
on many a hill,
And flying over Snake Alley
gives me a thrill!

The parks, oh the parks,
    where you can see every tree,
That grows in the state
    where I most love to be!

If I flew further east, I would be in Illinois.
But to me, Iowa's state bird, that would not be a joy.

Davenport

Another town north of here
I love to explore.
Is Davenport where Chiropractic's home
is close to the shore.

There's a lot to do here,
just fly over it with me,
Oh, the things you can do
and the places you can see!

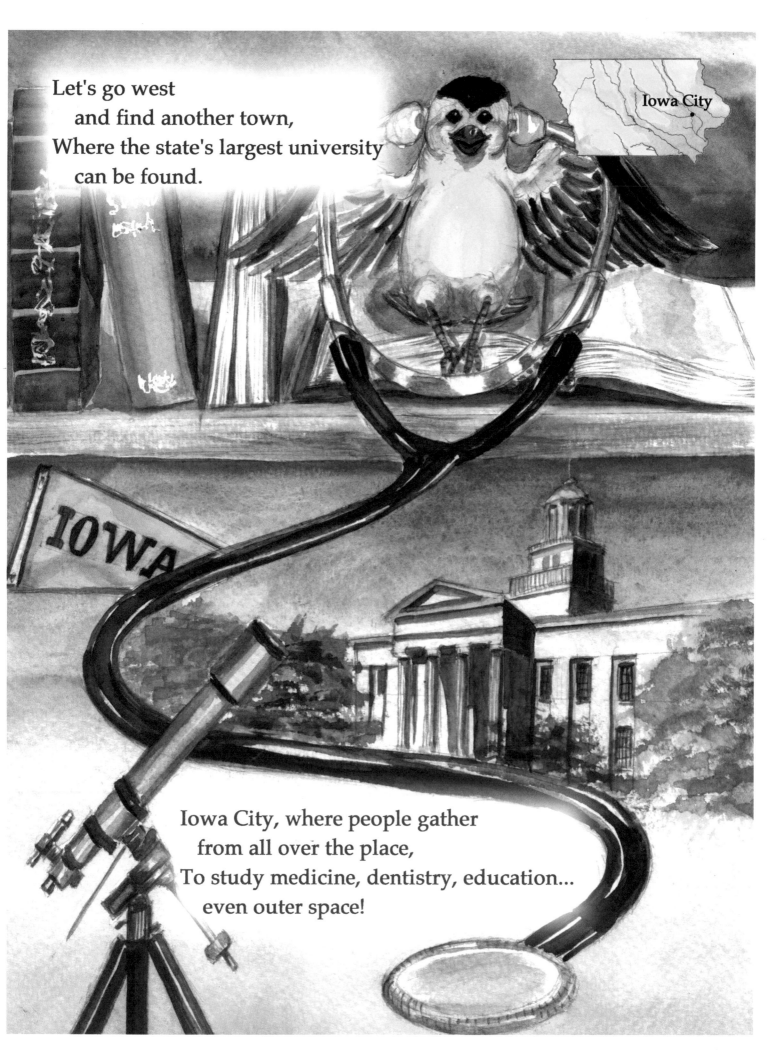

Let's go west
    and find another town,
Where the state's largest university
    can be found.

Iowa City

IOWA

Iowa City, where people gather
    from all over the place,
To study medicine, dentistry, education...
    even outer space!

City of Five Seasons

Cedar Rapids

Now join me and let's fly north to Cedar Rapids and see,
Where Czech immigrants founded a bustling community!

As we fly east to Dubuque, a unique hilly town,
You can have fun snow skiing at Sundown!

Down the hills they fly over the snow,
It is amazing to see just how fast they all go!

Dubuque

Right in the middle of the state is a city I like,
Students at the university there study
more than just Psych.

AMES

Ames

Ames is the place where they study animals like me,
They learn what we should eat and what makes us happy!

Another beautiful sight that no one should miss
Is Clear Lake where boating is high on my list.

Clear Lake

Ft. Dodge is a place of interest to me,
The rebuilt fort there is an exciting place you can see.

The surrounding farm land is as black as can be,
And the richest on earth most will agree!

Fort Dodge

Now let's travel west to the edge on the north,
Sioux City is a town from where Indians went forth.

Sioux City

Sioux City is where more popcorn is packaged by day,
than any other city in the whole U.S.A.

The city is near to South Dakota to the west,
But I prefer flying over Iowa, 'cause it's the state I like best!

Council Bluffs

Since I am flying on Iowa's west coast,
Join me down south in Council Bluffs where they boast,
Some of the highest bluffs in the state,
Where the view of the Missouri River is just great!

Just imagine how life used to be,
along Iowa's rivers where you see,
a steamboat puffing on a slow but steady cruise,
loaded with people, cargo and news.

Now come to the middle of the state
and you will see,
Many horse-drawn buggies
and children shouting with glee.

Kalona

I love to see how the Amish live there,
It's amazing, they don't drive in cars
to get anywhere.

They don't use electricity
in the area round Kalona,

and they use their own cows and pigs to make bologna!

Iowa is special because two rivers form its boundaries.
The Missouri and Mississippi are ideal
for barges and water skis!

There are hundreds of small towns in this rural state
with names like Winterset, Nashua, Walnut,
Elkader, LeClaire, Fort Madison, Mt. Pleasant and Storm Lake!

Now in between all these cities,
   if you look, you will find,
Farmers who work hard and have good crops
   on their minds.

The state is so beautiful and if you come with me,
You will see all the sites around Iowa and agree!!

Chamber of Commerce Offices in Iowa

City	Phone	City	Phone
Ackley	641-847-2234	Dewitt	563-659-8500
Adel	515-993-5472	Dubuque	563-557-9200
Albert City	712-843-5613	Durant	563-785-6099
Albia	641-932-5108	Dyersville	563-875-2311
Algona	515-295-7201	Eagle Grove	515-448-4821
Alta	712-732-7594	Eldora	641-939-3000
Altoona	515-967-3366	Eldridge	563-285-9965
Ames	515-232-2310	Elkader	563-245-2857
Anamosa	319-462-4879	Emmetsburg	712-852-2283
Ankeny	515-964-0685	Essex	712-379-3485
Arnolds Park	800-839-9987	Estherville	712-362-3541
Atlantic	712-243-3017	Fairfield	641-472-2111
Audubon	712-563-3780	Fayette	563-425-4316
Bancroft	515-885-2382	Forest City	641-585-2092
Bedford	712-523-3637	Fort Dodge	515-955-5500
Belle Plaine	319-444-2541	Fort Madison	319-372-5471
Bellevue	563-872-5830	Garner	641-923-3993
Belmond	641-444-3937	George	712-475-2884
Bettendorf	563-355-4753	Glenwood	712-527-3298
Bloomfield	641-664-1726	Greenfield	641-743-8444
Boone	800-266-6312	Grimes	515-986-5770
Britt	641-843-3867	Grinnell	641-236-6555
Burlington	800-82-RIVER	Griswold	712-778-4712
Carroll	712-792-4383	Grundy Center	319-825-3838
Cedar Falls	319-266-3593	Guthrie Center	641-747-8187
Cedar Rapids	319-398-5317	Guttenberg	877-252-2323
Centerville	800-611-3800	Hampton	641-456-5668
Chariton	641-774-4059	Harlan	888-876-1774
Charles City	641-228-4234	Hartley	712-728-2165
Cherokee	641-225-6414	Hawarden	712-551-4433
Clarinda	712-542-2166	Holstein	712-368-4368
Clarion	515-532-2256	Humboldt	515-332-1481
Clear Lake	800-285-5338	Hudson	319-988-4655
Clinton	563-242-5702	Ida Grove	712-364-3404
Colfax	515-674-3565	Independence	319-334-7178
Conrad	641-366-2165	Indianola	866-961-6269
Corning	641-332-3243	Iowa City	319-337-9637
Corydon	641-872-1338	Iowa Falls	641-648-5549
Council Bluffs	800-228-6878	Jefferson	515-386-2155
Cresco	800-373-6293	Jesup	319-827-3100
Creston	641-782-7021	Johnston	515-276-9064
Davenport	563-322-1706	Kalona	319-656-2660
Decorah	800-201-3458	Keokuk	319-524-5055
Denison	712-263-5621	Knoxville	641-828-7978
Des Moines	800-451-2625	La Porte City	319-342-3526
Laurens	712-845-2620	Lake City	712-464-7611
Le Claire	563-289-9970	Lake Mills	641-592-5253

Chamber of Commerce Offices in Iowa

City	Phone	City	Phone
Le Mars	712-546-8821	Rock Valley	712-476-9300
Lenox	641-333-4272	Rockwell	641-822-4906
Leon	641-446-6720	Rockwell City	712-297-8874
Logan	712-644-3208	Sac City	712-662-7316
Manchester	563-927-4141	Saint Ansgar	641-713-2140
Manning	712-655-3541	Schaller	712-275-4229
Manson	712-469-3311	Sheldon	712-324-2813
Maquoketa	563-652-4602	Shenandoah	712-246-3455
Marengo	319-741-5241	Sibley	712-754-3212
Marion	319-377-6316	Sidney	712-374-2801
Marshalltown	641-753-6645	Sigourney	641-622-2288
Mason City	641-423-5724	Sioux Center	712-722-3457
Massena	712-779-2295	Sioux City	712-255-7903
McGregor	800-896-0910	Spencer	712-262-5680
Missouri Valley	712-642-2553	Storm Lake	712-732-3780
Monona	563-539-4455	Story City	515-733-4214
Monticello	319-465-5626	Strawberry Point	563-933-4400
Mount Pleasant	800-436-7619	Stuart	515-523-2868
Mount Vernon	877-895-8214	Sumner	563-578-3419
Muscatine	563-263-8895	Tipton	563-886-6350
Nevada	800-558-2288	Toledo	641-484-6661
New Hampton	641-394-2021	Traer	319-478-2346
New London	319-367-2573	Tripoli	319-882-3595
Newton	641-792-5545	Urbandale	515-331-6855
Northwood	641-324-1810	Villisca	712-826-5222
Norwalk	515-981-0619	Vinton	319-472-3955
Odebolt	712-668-2243	Wall Lake	712-664-2311
Oelwein	319-283-1105	Washington	319-653-3272
Onawa	712-423-1801	Waterloo	319-233-8431
Orange City	712-707-4510	Waukee	515-978-7115
Osage	641-732-3163	Waukon	563-568-4110
Osceola	641-342-4200	Waverly	800-251-0360
Oskaloosa	641-672-2591	Webster City	515-832-2564
Ottumwa	641-682-3465	West Bend	515-887-2181
Panora	641-755-3300	West Branch	319-643-2111
Parkersburg	319-346-1147	West Des Moines	515-225-6009
Pella	888-746-3882	West Liberty	319-627-4876
Perry	515-465-4601	West Union	563-422-3070
Pleasant Hill	515-261-0466	Williamsburg	319-668-1500
Pleasantville	515-848-3903	Wilton	563-732-2330
Pocahontas	712-335-4841	Winfield	319-257-6661
Postville	563-864-7247	Winterset	800-298-6119
Red Oak	712-623-4821		
Remsen	712-786-2136		
Rock Rapids	712-472-3456		

ABOUT THE AUTHOR.....

Sharon Rexroth, a former Mrs. Iowa, wanted to teach her grandchildren about the state in which all of them live. Unable to find just the right book to capture their interest and spark their enthusiasm, she chose to show them Iowa through the eyes of the state bird, the goldfinch.

A goldfinch lends a unique and interesting perspective. With the help of her talented sister-in-law, Lee-Ann Paasch, she is able to impart true-to-life watercolor pictures which depict the flavor of Iowa and show the reader that Iowa is so much more than pigs and tall corn.

Sharon graduated from Iowa Wesleyan College in Mt. Pleasant, Iowa, with a degree in communications. She is a financial service representative for Allstate. Because of her love of children, she substitute teaches in the Burlington and West Burlington School Districts.

ABOUT THE ILLUSTRATOR.....

Lee-Ann Paasch graduated from Millikin University in Decatur, Illinois, and teaches elementary education in a church-affiliated school. She is married to Sharon's brother, Richard Paasch, pastor of Maranatha Baptist Church in Zolpho Springs, Florida.

This book works well for a family library, an on-a-trip diversion or a resource for use in private or public schools.

It is an excellent fundraiser and is available at discounts for multiple quantities.

Similar books for other states are in process.

Call us at 1-800-571-2665 for comments, information or for ordering.